The Loch Monster

by William Owen

with a Foreword by

David James M.B.E., D.S.C., M.P.

JARROLD COLOUR PUBLICATIONS · NORWICH

Le Loch Ness est célèbre dans le monde entier pour son monstre. Ce lac contient le plus grand volume d'eau douce de toutes les Iles Britanniques et est profond d'au moins 210 mètres. Une colonie de monstres pourrait donc y vivre sans être détectée ni dérangée.

Autant qu'on le sache, le monstre fut aperçu pour la première fois en l'an 565 par Adamnan qui raconte, dans son Histoire de St Colomba, comment la bête tua un homme. On n'en entendit plus parler pendant plus de 1.000 ans, mais en 1930 il y eut un reportage dans la presse sur trois pêcheurs qui avaient aperçu le monstre. Cet article en provoqua de nombreux autres, mais c'est en 1933 seulement qu'on réussit à prendre une photographie du monstre.

Depuis, de nombreuses expéditions ont tenté de prouver l'existence des monstres, mais le lac est si profond et troublé qu'il est pratiquement impossible de prendre des photographies sous-marines. En 1975, cependant, le docteur Robert Rines prit certaines photographies où l'on peut deviner une forme qui ressemble à la tête et la nageoire d'un monstre.

Loch Ness in Schottland ist weltberühmt durch sein Monster. Der See hat die größte Menge Süßwasser in Großbritannien und ist wenigstens 260 Meter tief und wäre somit ein ideales Revier für eine Familie von Ungeheuern, wo sie ungestört und unentdeckt leben könnten.

Das Monster wurde zum erstenmal A.D. 565 erwähnt, als Adamnan in seiner Biografie des St. Columba beschreibt, wie es einen Mann tötet. Dann hörte man über tausend Jahre lang nichts, bis im Jahre 1930 der erste Zeitungsartikel über ein Monster, das drei Angler gesehen haben wollten, abgedruckt wurde. Diesem Bericht folgten viele andere, aber im Jahre 1933 erst wurde eine Fotografie gemacht.

Seitdem haben verschiedene Expeditionen versucht, die Existenz der Monsters beweisen, aber der See ist so tief und dunkel, daß Unterwasserfotografie fast unmöglich ist. Im Jahre 1975 jedoch gelangen Dr. Robert Rines Aufnahmen, die möglicherweise den Kopf und die Flosse des Monsters zeigen.

Foreword

It is a pleasure to write a foreword to William Owen's well-informed booklet about Loch Ness. He rightly divides his readers into three groups – firm believers, those who won't believe until they are bitten by a 'Monster' and those who retain an open mind. Very properly he adopts the objective stance.

I have spent many weeks by the lochside – and many blood-chilling hours drifting around Urquhart Bay on flat-calm nights praying for (and dreading) a close-up surfacing – without ever seeing anything. All the same I must admit I am a firm believer, viewing the evidence in its totality.

I have talked to scores of eye-witnesses, nine of whom have had chance encounters at ranges of feet rather than yards, usually while out fishing. I have sent four sequences of moving film to the R.A.F. photographic interpretation unit, all of which have indicated fast-moving objects larger than any Northern Hemisphere Seal. I have sponsored three separate sonar-probes, which have shown objects moving in the middle depths, which are difficult to explain away. Finally I was with Dr Robert Rines on the night when he obtained his underwater 'flipper' photographs.

If there were hundreds of people of a highly responsible character, who were prepared to attest that they had met an individual and if over the years a dagger, a pistol and a phial of arsenic had been found, would a jury fail to convict simply because no body had been recovered?

However, the readers are the jury and I must desist from further special pleading.

Urquhart Castle overlooks Urquhart Bay on the north shore of Loch Ness.
Le château d'Urquhart, sur la rive du Loch Ness, domine la baie du même nom.
Urquhart Castle überblickt Urquhart Bay am nördlichen Ufer von Loch Ness.

Scotland's
Loch Ness Monster.

Loch Ness is well known throughout the world as the home of the famous Loch Ness Monster and because of this attracts a large number of visitors. But had the Monster never been heard of the loch itself would always have been an attraction, if only because it is set in some of the most beautiful mountain scenery in the world.

The waters of Loch Ness fill part of the Great Glen. 'Glen' is a Gaelic word meaning a narrow valley. The Great Glen was formed many millions of years ago by some gigantic movement in the earth's crust. The earth split open and a great valley was created cutting diagonally across the country from coast to coast. Much more recently, after the ice-age glaciers had scraped and shaped this great valley and its surrounding mountains into their present form, water filled its greatest depths and three narrow lochs were formed. Loch Ness in the northeast, Loch Oich in the middle and Loch Lochy in the southwest. Loch Ness is the longest and by far the deepest of the three lochs. It covers an area of 14,000 acres or 21¾ square miles: Its length is 24 miles (38·4 km), and the average width is 1 mile (1·6 km). The depth in the centre for most of its length is 700 feet (213 m), and although the maximum depth is not known precisely, it has been stated to be 820 feet (250 m). However, in 1969 a submarine found that instruments on board showed an even greater depth than this at a spot off Urquhart Castle.

The loch contains a volume of freshwater which has been estimated as 263 billion cubic feet (7 billion cu m). This far exceeds any other loch in Great Britain and is three times the volume of water in Loch Lomond although Loch

The Caledonian Canal, seen here at Fort Augustus, is sixty miles long.
Le Canal Calédonien, long de 97 kilomètres, est pris ici à Fort Augustus.
Der Kaledonische Kanal, hier bei Fort Augustus, ist 97 Kilometer lang.

The A82 road runs along Loch Ness from Inverness to Fort Augustus.
La route A82, d'Inverness à Fort Augustus, longe les bords du Loch Ness.
Die A82 verläuft am Ufer des Loch Ness von Inverness bis Fort Augustus.

Lomond covers a much larger area. The surface of the loch is 52 feet above sea level, whereas the greater part of the floor of the loch is well below sea level. The surface level can rise very rapidly during periods of heavy rain or when snow thaws on surrounding hills. A rise of two feet within a few hours is commonplace and a rise of seven feet has frequently been recorded.

Loch Ness is fed by eight rivers and about forty burns or streams. Only one river at the Inverness end carries away the overflow from the loch into the North Sea.

The loch never freezes owing to its great depth. The surface water which is in contact with the air, cools and becomes heavier than the water below, therefore it sinks and is replaced by the warmer water rising to the surface. The action is continuous and renders the freezing of the surface impossible. The temperature of the deepest parts of the loch changes but a few degrees during winter or summer. In winter the surrounding atmosphere is warmed by the loch, consequently the roads along the shores seldom retain ice and snow for very long.

Most of the northern shore of the loch has been easily accessible since 1933 when a new road was constructed between Fort Augustus and Inverness. This road, the A82, follows closely the shore of the loch only leaving the lochside to loop inland at the villages of Drumnadrochit and Invermoriston in order to cross the rivers which flow through these villages. The narrow ledge upon which the road is built was blasted from the steep rocky shoreline, so that for much of its length the road is flanked on one side by a steep rockface and on the other by a sheer drop to the waters of the loch.

Much of the southern shore of the loch is not so easily accessible. The military road built on this side of the loch before 1730 by General Wade linked the military forts in the Great Glen. The road follows a route well away from the loch until it reaches the village of Foyers. The steepness of the hills between Fort Augustus and Foyers did not permit of its construction closer to the loch, the main obstacle being the aptly named Beinn a' Bhacairdh or 'The Hindrance', a mountain with a height of 1,812 feet. On the northwestern flank a semi-circular area of scree on the hillside, called locally 'The Horseshoe', drops steeply into the loch. Underwater the hill continues to drop away just as steeply, and a depth of 236 feet has been recorded only 100 feet from the shore.

The village of Fort Augustus lies at the extreme south-western end of the loch and from a spot just outside the village one can obtain an uninterrupted view down the entire length of the loch. The village takes its name from the fort which was built here in 1727 by General Wade and named after the king's son, William Augustus. The fort was captured and damaged by the army of Bonnie Prince

Fort Augustus and its Abbey lie at the south-western tip of Loch Ness.
Fort Augustus et son abbaye sont situés à la pointe sud-ouest du lac.
Fort Augustus mit seiner Abtei liegt am südwestlichen Zipfel von Loch Ness.

Loch Ness is one of three lochs forming part of the Caledonian Canal system.
Le Loch Ness est l'un des trois lacs faisant partie du Canal Calédonien.
Loch Ness ist einer der drei Seen im Kaledonischen Kanalsystem.

Charlie in 1746. Later the buildings were repaired and a small garrison remained in occupation until 1854. Today Fort Augustus Abbey stands on the site of the fort and some of the fort buildings are incorporated into the present structure.

Two rivers, the Oich and the Tarff flow into Loch Ness at Fort Augustus and here too the Caledonian Canal joins Loch Ness. The canal links together the three lochs in the Great Glen allowing seagoing vessels to travel from the North Sea to the Atlantic Ocean. The canal was constructed under the supervision of the celebrated engineer Thomas Telford. The several stretches of canalway add up to twenty-two miles but the complete journey is over sixty miles because it includes the lengths of Loch Ness, Loch Oich and Loch Lochy. The highest loch of the three is Loch Oich which is 105 feet above sea level. Loch Lochy is

93 feet above sea level and Loch Ness 52 feet above sea level, consequently the differences in heights meant that a series of locks had to be constructed.

Beside the canal locks in Fort Augustus is The Great Glen Exhibition which is a modern style museum and audio/visual show which tells the history of the Great Glen. The exhibition also includes information on Loch Ness and the Monster.

About one mile outside Fort Augustus in Inchnacardoch Bay is the only island in Loch Ness. Today the island is known as 'Cherry Island' but its Gaelic name is Eilean Muireach – 'Murdochs Island'. The island is man-made having been built to hold a small fort. There are several other similar islands in the Great Glen. The island was built on a flooring of oak beams that prevent the rubble of which it is constructed from sinking into the floor of the loch. Originally the island was much larger than it is today, measuring 180 feet by 168 feet at the water's edge. When the Caledonian Canal was built the level of Loch Ness was raised by nine feet, so that much of the island is now beneath the water.

There are several strange phenomena which intrigue people today; unidentified flying objects or flying saucers; the 'Big Foot' of North America, which is supposed to be some kind of missing link in man's evolution; another is the Loch Ness Monster. On the subject of the Loch Ness Monster people seem to fit into one of three distinct categories. There are those who firmly believe because they have seen for themselves, or who believe despite the fact that they have not had first-hand experience of the phenomenon. Secondly, there are those who do not believe and will not believe until a monster jumps out of the loch and bites them. I think it is a pity that there are not more people in a third category, that is people who wait to be convinced one way or the other by concrete evidence.

Six miles from Fort Augustus is the delightful glen of Glenmoriston.
A 10 kilomètres de Fort Augustus se trouve la charmante vallée de Glenmoriston.
Zehn Kilometer von Fort Augustus entfernt liegt das reizende Glenmoriston-Tal.

Cherry Island near Fort Augustus, the only island in Loch Ness, is man-made.
En face de Fort Augustus se trouve Cherry Island, créée artificiellement.
Cherry Island nahe Fort Augustus ist von Menschenhand geschaffen.

The River Moriston flows into Loch Ness below Invermoriston.
La Moriston se jette dans le lac au nord, près d'Invermoriston.
Der fluß Moriston mündet unterhalb Invermoriston in den Loch Ness.

I hope that I fit this third category. I have lived close by
the loch for fifteen years and for the past seven of these in a
cottage only a few yards from the water's edge. In that time
I have seen many things which could have been mistaken
for the Monster, but these things have always turned out to
be something else, floating three trunks or barrels or
animals swimming in the loch. I once saw a red deer stag
swim ashore near Allt Saidh three miles from Invermoriston.
On another occasion, while travelling to Inverness at a
point where the road is perhaps seventy feet above the loch
I saw what appeared to be three undulating humps. I
watched fascinated as they travelled through the water at
about the same speed as I was travelling along the road. It
was wintertime and the sky was grey and the waters of the
loch were dark. I was almost convinced that I was watching
a large animal until the first hump appeared to rise up from

the water, split into three parts and become three dark-backed geese which had been flying in single file close to one another and close to the surface. From above and against the dark and broken water they had appeared as one. The geese continued to rise until they were high above the water to form a V formation and continue their journey.

I do not regard it as surprising that I have not seen the Monster and it does not make me dismiss the possibility of there being such a creature in Loch Ness. There are many people who have lived all their lives beside the loch who do not claim to have seen it, and yet there are those who after perhaps forty years or more of never having seen anything unusual will suddenly declare that they have had a sighting and that they are now utterly convinced. I still hope that one day I shall have a close and unmistakable sighting, and that I shall have my camera with me when I do.

The earliest recorded sighting of the Loch Ness Monster

This unusual ripple was photographed by Mrs Jessie Tait of Inverness in 1969.
Cette ondulation très curieuse fut photographiée en 1969 par Madame Jessie Tait.
Diese ungewöhnliche Wellenkräuselung wurde 1969 von Mrs Tait fotografiert.

was in AD 565. It was narrated by Adamnan in his biography of St Columba. The Monster was supposed to have attacked and killed a man who was swimming in the River Ness. It was a very long time before anything more was written about the existence of a monster in Loch Ness – almost 1,400 years.

The first newspaper to print a report on the 'Monster' appears to have been the *Northern Chronicle* on 27 August 1930. Three young men from Inverness were out fishing in a boat on the loch when they observed a great commotion in the water about 600 yards off. The strange disturbance approached to within about 300 yards of their boat. Spray was being thrown high in the air but still they could make out some kind of body which they described as being about 20 feet long and 3 feet or so out of the water. The wash it created had caused their boat to rock violently, and the three men were convinced that what they had seen was a

Left: The mountain scenery around Loch Ness is seen here from the Dores road.
À gauche: Le paysage autour du Loch Ness est vu ici de la route de Dores.
Links: Von der Straße kann man diese Berglandschaft um Loch Ness herum genießen.

Right: Sir Peter Scott, a Director of the Loch Ness Investigation Bureau.
À droite: Sir Peter Scott, un directeur du Bureau d'Investigations du Loch Ness.
Rechts: Sir Peter Scott, einer der Direktoren des Loch-Ness-Forschungsbüros.

living creature. A request by the newspaper for further information on the phenomenon brought several letters from people who themselves had had similar experiences.

The *Inverness Courier*, on 2 May 1933, published a report of a sighting by a Mr and Mrs Mackay from Drumnadrochit, who had seen something strange in the water while motoring along the north shore of the loch near Abriachan.

These early newspaper reports sparked off a great many others so that by the end of 1933 as many as thirty reports had appeared in local newspapers. The national papers and the B.B.C. were quick to follow up with reports.

So far no photographs had been obtained of the phenomenon although on 12 August 1933 the *Scottish Daily Express* reported that a certain Captain Ellisford, a well-known amateur photographer, had arrived in Inverness with a large box of modern photographic equipment including a telephoto lens, en route for Loch Ness. However, it seems that the captain had no success. The first man to obtain a photograph was a local man, Mr Hugh Gray an employee of the British Aluminium Company's factory at Foyers.

After church one Sunday morning Mr Gray went for a stroll by the lochside close to where the River Foyers pours into the loch. The sun was shining and the loch was like a millpond when an object of considerable dimensions rose up out of the water close to the shore. Mr Gray was carrying a camera and he managed to take five shots before the object sank out of sight. The photograph appeared in the *Daily Sketch* on 6 December 1933 together with a statement by Kodak employees that the negative had not been tampered with.

It was at the end of 1933 also that the first motion picture was obtained which claimed to show the 'Monster'. Mr Malcolm Irvine of Scottish Film Productions had stationed a small team of cameramen around the loch. After a fruitless vigil of two weeks duration Mr Irvine observed some movement in the water only 100 yards away from his camera position, which was on a hillside opposite Urquhart Castle. The film obtained ran for less than a minute and showed some unidentifiable object moving along at about 9 to 10 m.p.h. leaving a trail of foam. Interesting but not at all helpful in determining what manner of beast inhabited the loch.

The *Daily Mail* announced that it was to engage a famous big-game hunter to track down the Monster. The hunter concentrated his search along the shores of the loch, consequently some local prankster planted footprints in soft sand for the hunter to find using the mounted hind foot of a hippopotamus. The big-game hunter took the bait hook, line and sinker, and the *Daily Mail* appeared with the headline 'Monster of Loch Ness is not a Legend but a Fact.' Casts were taken of the prints and subsequently examined by experts at the British Museum of Natural History who of

The Falls of Foyers plunge down the hillside on the southern shore of the loch.
Les chutes de Foyers tombent du haut d'une colline sur la berge sud du lac.
Der Foyers-Wasserfall stürzt am Südufer des Sees den Berghang hinunter.

One of the deepest parts of the loch lies just off Urquhart Castle.
L'un des endroits les plus profonds du lac, juste au large du château d'Urquhart.
Eine der tiefsten Stellen im See befindet sich querab Urquhart Castle.

This photograph of the Monster was taken by R. K. Wilson in 1934.
Cette photographie du monstre fut prise par R. K. Wilson en 1934.
Diese Aufnahme des Monsters wurde 1934 von R. K. Wilson gemacht.

course identified them for what they were. From then on many other practical jokers tried to get in on the act. Anything that would float was pressed into service, barrels, motor tyres, upturned boats. But some went to greater lengths than this. Elaborate models were constructed and set afloat in the loch.

The first photograph to show the head and neck of the Monster was taken by a London gynaecologist, Mr R. K. Wilson, in April 1934 (see opposite). He took four photographs using a plate camera. When these were developed two were found to be blank, the third showed the head and neck, and the fourth showed the head sinking into the water. Mr Wilson did not claim to have photographed the Monster, he merely said that he had photographed an object moving in Loch Ness.

In this same year, 1934, there were several organised research efforts the most notable of which was that led by Sir Edward Mountain. Twenty unemployed men were signed up at the Inverness Labour Exchange. Each man was equipped with a simple box·camera and a pair of binoculars. Several photographs were taken but these merely showed vague shapes in the loch, and the party departed without having reached any conclusions.

In July 1951 a photograph was taken by Mr Lachlan Stuart, a local woodsman, who lived on the south side of the loch opposite Urquhart Bay. Mr Stuart had got up about 6.30 a.m. to milk the cow when from his window he saw what he first thought to be a boat moving at speed along the middle of the loch towards Dores. The object appeared to Mr Stuart to be moving faster than the boats he was used to seeing on the loch and this made him pay more attention to it. As he watched another object appeared behind the first. Mr Stuart called his wife and a friend who was staying with them, and the three went down to the shore. By the time they had reached the water's edge a third hump had

Urquhart Bay has been the scene of many sightings of the Monster.
C'est de la baie d'Urquhart que le monstre a été aperçu de nombreuses fois.
In Urquhart Bay ist das Monster oft gesehen worden.

appeared on the surface and all three objects had moved closer to the shore. Mr Stuart focused his camera on the three humps and took a photograph (see opposite). Mr Stuart said later that he had seen a long thin neck and a head about the size of a sheep's head lying flat on the water.

In July 1955 Mr P. A. MacNab, returning from a holiday in the north, stopped his car above Urquhart Castle in order to take a photograph of the castle itself when he saw something in the water below the castle. He quickly took a photograph using an Exacta 127 camera with a six-inch lens (see overleaf).

Over the years there have been many one-man research efforts but perhaps none more persistent than that by Tim Dinsdale. In 1960 Mr Dinsdale took a 16 mm film of a large hump travelling through the water at speed. The object followed a zig-zag course until it eventually submerged. For comparison Mr Dinsdale filmed a 15 foot boat fitted with a 5 h.p. motor travelling over the same course. There was quite a lot of difference in the size of the two wakes, that of the 'Monster' being much the larger of the two.

Since 1960 there has been a succession of monster-hunting expeditions and many different types of modern technical equipment have been brought into use. In 1962 the Loch Ness Investigation Bureau was formed with David James M.P., Constance Whyte, Peter Scott and Richard Fitter as its directors. The bureau proposed to act as a clearing house for information and also as a research body. In the beginning the bureau was only involved in active research for a few weeks each summer. By 1964, however, they had established a more permanent headquarters beside the loch at Achnahannet. Camera stations were positioned at different points around the loch. These were equipped with both still and ciné cameras fitted with powerful telephoto lenses. Eventually several vans were purchased to create a fleet of mobile camera stations. Apart from surface photography many other ideas were tried. Ex-War Department searchlights each with a range of six miles played upon the surface of the loch every night for two

These three distinct humps were photographed by Mr Lachlan Stuart in 1951.
Sur cette photographie de M. Lachlan Stuart, prise en 1951, on voit trois bosses.
Diese drei deutlichen Höcker wurden 1951 von Mr Lachlan Stuart fotografiert.

weeks in the hope that the 'Monster' would be attracted to the surface. Underwater listening devices were tried. Echo sounders and biological experiments, airborne searches using an Autogyro, hot-air balloons, infra-red night cameras, sonar scanners and submarines. Although the experiments carried out have taught us more about the loch than was known hitherto, none of them have as yet produced irrefutable evidence of the existence of a family of monsters in Loch Ness. Oh yes! If there is one monster then there must be at least twenty, or so say the biologists. It does stand to reason that one solitary monster could not have lived trapped in the loch for thousands of years. Therefore, if there are monsters in the loch, there must be a breeding herd of them.

In 1969 a film company arrived at Loch Ness to shoot scenes for the feature film *The Private Life of Sherlock Holmes*. One scene in the script called for shots of the Loch Ness Monster. The studio workshops built a life-size model of the Monster which was transported to the loch. It was to be towed through the water by a small submarine. Unfortunately the model accidentally sank in Urquhart Bay. As it would have taken too long to recover it from the bottom of the bay, the film company abandoned it. With much of the effort now concentrated on underwater research it is possible that this model monster may show up on sonar charts and on photographs taken underwater.

At the end of 1972 the Loch Ness Investigation Bureau was forced to close down owing to lack of funds and because it was unable to obtain planning approval from Inverness-shire County Council to continue in occupation of the Achnahannet site. American scientific organisations had worked with the Loch Ness Investigation Bureau, and since the bureau closed down these American organisations have continued their work. The most active of the organisations has been The Academy of Applied Science under its president Dr Robert Rines. In 1971 an Academy team

Urquhart Castle provides the setting for P. A. MacNab's 1955 photograph.
Le château d'Urquhart fournit le décor de cette photographie.
Urquhart Castle ist der Hintergrund für P. MacNabs Aufnahme.

Tim Dinsdale is one of the most dedicated researchers of the Monster.
Tim Dinsdale, l'un des chasseurs de monstres les plus dévoués.
Tim Dinsdale ist einer der eifrigsten Monster-Forscher.

A Loch Ness Investigation Bureau camera station. *Right:* The 8 a.m. watch.
Un poste d'observation photographique du Bureau d'Investigations du Loch Ness.
Eine Kamerastation des Loch-Ness-Forschungsbüros. *Rechts:* Die 8-Uhr-Wache.

Until its closure, the Bureau's headquarters were at Achnahannet.
Le quartier général du Bureau se trouvait autrefois à Achnahannet.
Das Hauptquartier des Forschungsbüros befand sich in Achnahannet.

brought an underwater stroboscopic camera to the loch. This equipment was designed by Professor Harold Edgerton of the Massachusetts Institute of Technology who has made equipment for that famous underwater explorer Jacques Cousteau. The equipment consists of two water-tight cylinders, one containing a 16 mm camera and the other a powerful electronic flash gun. The camera is synchronised with the flashing light so that one frame is exposed with each flash of light. The camera was lowered on to the floor of the loch in Urquhart Bay. That year the equipment was in operation for only a two-week period and did not produce any results. The team returned the following year and this time the camera was linked to a Raytheon Sonar unit. The equipment operates in such a way that should a large under-water object enter the sonar beam, the camera and its flashing light are triggered, and hopefully pictures of the object are obtained.

Murray Barber is seen here with a mobile camera station at Abriachan.
Murray Barber à Abriachan, avec un poste d'observation photographique mobile.
Hier sieht man Murray Barber mit einer Kamerastation bei Abriachan.

In the early hours of 8 August the equipment was operating under the waters of Urquhart Bay when a large object entered the sonar beam and was photographed. Underwater photography is difficult in the loch because of peat particles that are suspended in the water, and a bright light does not penetrate very far but is reflected back by these particles. However, when the developed film was examined it was obvious that something had been photographed although it was impossible to tell exactly what. To improve the pictures they were sent for computer processing to the N.A.S.A. computer enhancement experts who processed the Apollo moon photographs. After treatment one photograph revealed what appears to be a flipper, optical measurements of which showed it to be six to eight feet long and from two to four feet in width (see overleaf). Even this photograph has not succeeded in convincing the world of the existence of a monster.

A mobile camera unit with both still and ciné cameras at Fort Augustus.
On voit ici à Fort Augustus une unité photographique mobile.
Eine Kamerawache mit Fotoapparaten und Filmkameras bei Fort Augustus.

Dr Robert Rines and his team on a Loch Ness Investigation Bureau boat.
Le docteur Rines sur un bateau du Bureau d'Investigations du Loch Ness.
Dr. Robert Rines und seine Mannschaft in einem Boot des Forschungsbüros.

Dr Rines continued to operate his equipment during the summer months of 1973 and 1974, but it was not until the following summer that another series of pictures was obtained. When news of these photographs was given to the press in November 1975 it created something of a sensation throughout the world. One of the pictures was a close-up of the Monster's head which had two horn-like appendages and an open mouth with large teeth. This could also be a description of the fibreglass model which sank in Urquhart Bay. How many people will accept these pictures as proof of the existence of a monster in Loch Ness is anybody's guess. Only one thing is certain, there will continue to be three groups of people, the believers, the non-believers and those who say "I'll wait and see".

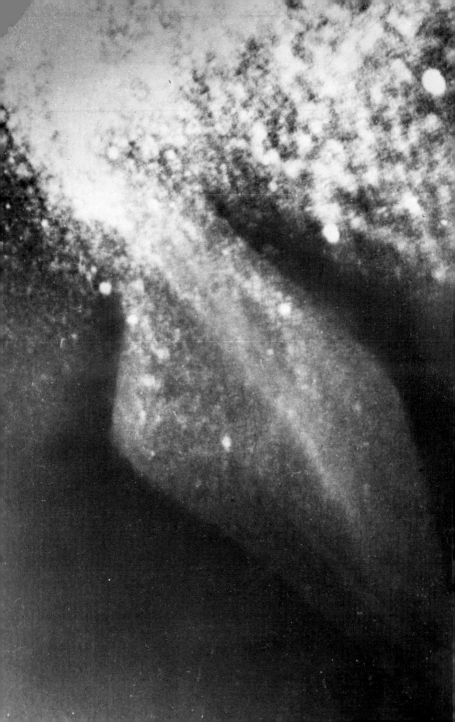

Recent Developments, by Gilbert Summers

After 1975, the general feeling from those parties actively seeking a solution to the monster mystery was that a painstaking and scientific approach was the only course to follow. Thus the 'euphoria' and wild claims of the 1960s, with their sometimes extremely dubious photographic evidence, gave way to a less spectacular but more cautious approach. The pictorial evidence from the 1960s seemed to show that it was extremely difficult to film the phenomenon on the surface, while the 1975 pictures certainly indicated the problems of obtaining clear photographic evidence underwater. The mid-1970s images seem now to have been among the last pieces of pictorial evidence to be submitted for scientific or public verdict. Meanwhile controversy continued into the 1980s over exactly what Dr Rines had photographed on a June night in 1975, in the peat-fogged murk forty feet down, with the camera rocked as if by a large moving object. Particularly disturbing is the single frame that was to be dubbed the 'gargoyle head' and one of a number of underwater pictures on display at the Loch Ness Monster Exhibition at Drumnadrochit.

At the same time, it was gradually dawning on a wider public that, in a curious way, the more cameras that were trained above the water, the less evidence appeared within range. Nessie remained extremely camera-shy, on the surface. Searching in the depths had to be the way forward to a real solution, which the 1975 pictures had by no means provided. But in the early 1980s, even more modern equipment was to produce its own significant, though at first sight unspectacular, evidence.

This underwater photograph by Dr Rines shows a flipper-like image.
On distingue sur cette photographie une forme ressemblant à une nageoire.
Diese Unterwasseraufnahme von Dr. Rines zeigt einem flossenähnlichen Umriß.

The main lead in investigations was taken by the Loch Ness and Morar Project. Their philosophy was simple, their approach admirably cautious. First, find some evidence that the unexplored depths of the loch could provide both a habitat and a food-source for the kind of large aquatic organism which was suggested by nearly fifty years of sightings. Thus, investigations of the deep basin floor revealed a stable environment of unchanging temperature (5·5 °C), no shortage of oxygen, great pressure (22 kg/sq. cm) and total darkness. More significantly, in addition to the echo-sounder evidence of an abundant fish population widespread to a depth of at least thirty metres, the Project actually caught char, a member of the salmon family, at a depth of 220 m.

This was taken as encouraging, as was the identification of other specimens taken at great depth, which incuded tiny mussels, copepods, worms and the larvae of midges. (The last of these confirms what many tourists have known for years – that there is no escape from Scottish midges, if they can survive on the bed of the loch at 220 m.) More seriously, attempts were then made to track, using sonar equipment, deep-water objects, already indicated by other expeditions' findings, particularly Birmingham University's in 1968.

The Loch Ness and Morar Project's vessels patrolled the loch in the summer months. The central trench of the loch was scanned by sonar on a twenty-four-hour basis with the most spectacular results being obtained in May 1982. The instrument used recorded its findings not on a paper trace but on magnetic tape with a visual display on a cathode screen. Even more importantly, the screen showed different colours, depending on the strength of the returning signal. These echoes from any kind of mid-water object are usually caused by reflections of air trapped within the target itself. Thus the small gas-filled swim bladder in fish will reflect the sonar's signal, as will the lungs of air breathers. Oddly enough, living tissue itself is a poor reflector as its density is close to that of water.

In a determined effort to approach the whole exercise as cautiously as possible, the project team also calibrated its equipment in a number of ways, learning to recognise freak echoes from the sides of the loch as well as attempting to track a plastic air-filled buoy. This seven-and-a-half-inch air-filled sphere presented a large target to the sonar, but was found to be extremely difficult to detect when suspended in mid water unless directly below the tracking boat.

After many trials confirmed that shoals of fish, for instance, would give recognisably different kinds of echoes from those received from individual targets, the Project team recorded more than forty contacts that they considered to be of interest in more than 1,500 hours patrolling of the deep central basin. With the calibration sphere on screen for comparison, the team, for example, recorded a target off Urquhart Castle, which they tracked for 68 seconds as it dived from 69 m to 111 m into the blackness of the loch. The strength of signal, depth of target and its vertical movement, the last being un-characteristic of shoaling fish, all point to what a single, large animate organism *would* look like, supposing such a creature existed.

The Project makes no more claims for the results than that. The possibility of unknown characteristics of the complex tracking technology causing these effects is, perhaps, just possible – in spite of a level of expertise and control features that suggest a real target of an unknown nature. Nevertheless, the research is indicative of a new ultra-cautious approach. Most interestingly of all, the next stage is to return to trying for underwater pictures of the tracked objects. This is the direction of research for the rest of the decade. Arguably, if pictures are obtained by this method, then they are likely to be of inanimate objects, given the camera-shy track record of the phenomenon so far. The project would then submit that even negative evidence of this kind would be highly significant – lifeless objects stay put to be photographed, while living creatures tend to swim away, consciously or otherwise avoiding man-made artefacts suspended in their otherwise peaceful environment.

Thus modern technology might yet solve the riddle of the loch. The popular press has had a long wait for the final indisputable picture – cathode-ray traces may excite the scientist but leave the average visitor unimpressed – but the tale has by no means ended. This strange, dark loch has not yet revealed all its secrets.

Acknowledgments

The author and publishers are deeply indebted to the following for their great help and co-operation in compiling this publication:

Dr Robert Rines, President of the Academy of Applied Science, Boston, Mass., U.S.A.
Sir Peter Scott
David James, M.B.E., D.S.C., M.P., Executive Director of the Loch Ness Investigation Bureau
The London Express News and Features Service
The Field Magazine

Photographs:
William Owen (pp. 1, 6 *top and bottom*, 9, 11 *bottom*,17, 18 *top*, 20, 23 *bottom*)
P. A. MacNab (p. 23 *top*)
D. Pattison (pp. 24 *top left and right*, 25, 26)
Dick Raynor (pp. 24 *bottom*, 27)
Dr Robert Rines (p. 28)
Lachlan Stuart (p. 21)
Jessie Tate (p. 13)
R. K. Wilson (p. 18 *bottom*)

Published by Jarrold Colour Publications, Norwich
Printed in Great Britain by Jarrold Printing, Norwich 6/89